COLOURFUL PEBBLES

Verses from the Learnings of Life

SHEETAL AGARWAL

INDIA • SINGAPORE • MALAYSIA

ISBN 979-8-88641-684-8

Dedicated to my daughter who is instrumental in bringing out the poet hidden in me, and in making me believe.

Contents

Acknowledgement..7

Introduction 8

1. You Came in My Life 11

2. Gratitude Fills My Heart 12

3. Designations.................................. 14

4. Me? A Writer?................................ 16

5. Guruji 18

6. Words.. 20

7. I Write... 22

8. Entitlement................................... 24

9. Writing and Me.............................. 25

10. You... 26

11. I Close My Eyes 28

12. The Pain Melted Away...................... 30

13. I Look For Success.......................... 32

14. The Burden of Attachments 34

15. Let Go of the Ego........................... 36

16. Comfort Zone 38

17. Giving... 39

18. Equanimity 40

19. Identify the Ego 41

20. Power of Empathy 42

21. Who Am I? 43

22. Metta 44

23. Mudita 46

24. Ebbs and Flows 48

25. Explore the Grey 50

26. Put Yourself First.. 52

27. Spirituality.. 54

28. Learning.. 56

29. Colours of the Pandemic 58

30. Why Judge? 60

31. Parental Paradox... 62

32. Stories 64

33. Script of Life.. 66

34. Seeking Validation... 68

35. Feminism 70

36. God and Me 72

37. Expectations versus Hope...................................... 74

38. Black Swan Events... 76

39. You Are the Key 78

40. Impermanence.. 79

41. Birthdays.. 80

42. Mother's Love 81

43. Motherhood 82

44. Stripped off Her Dignity 84

45. Being Old 86

46. Conflicted 88

47. Rights and Wrongs................................. 90

48. Reinvent.. 92

49. Experiences 93

50. Listening 94

51. When Our Gods Look Down..................... 95

52. Raising a Child 96

53. Journalists.. 97

54. Girl versus Boy 98

55. Stay in the Present 99

56. Imperfections 100

57. Purpose 102

58. I See You 104

59. Subtle Passion 106

60. Punctuations of Life............................... 108

61. Avoid the Noise 110

62. Love 111

63. Silence.. 112

64. You and I 114

65. Am I Doing Enough? 116

66. Alive Again 118

67. Stand Up for Yourself 119

68. What's Real? 120

69. Our True Love 122

70. The Sustainability Agenda 124

71. Analysing Life 126

72. I Wonder 128

73. Reacting or Responding 130

74. Silent Supporters 131

75. A Householder Hermit 132

76. Lockdown Tales 134

77. Lockdown Memoir 136

78. Craving and Aversion 139

79. Love Songs 140

80. I Surrender 142

Acknowledgement

I extend a heartfelt note of thanks to my parents (Mr. Ishwar Bansal and Mrs. Manju Bansal) who have always encouraged me to chart my own path. Due to their support and guidance, I have been able to chase my dreams and live life to the fullest. My husband, Vinay has stood by me through life's thick and thin. Over the years, he has become my true partner, and my go-to person in good times and bad. My daughter, Nitara, continues to inspire me every day. My brother, Amit has been supportive of me always. I am grateful to each one of them for being a part of my life and helping me move forward.

Introduction

Our thoughts and personalities are often a culmination of our life's experiences. Usually, every individual witnesses some life-changing milestones which define his/her way of living. There have been two such instances in my life. One, when I took my very first 10-day course of Vipassana, back in June 2016 and two, when we were blessed with a child in 2021, in the 13th year of our marriage.

Vipassana technique, as taught by venerable S.N. Goenka, in the tradition of Sayagyi U Ba Khin, changed my perspective of life completely. It was an eye opener for me, in multiple ways, and helped clear several doubts from my mind. Since then, I have attended two more 10-day courses, served in one 10-day course and practised the technique regularly. This technique has helped me know more about myself and the world around me. It has helped me become a calmer, better person. These are just the initial steps and my journey of self-discovery and self-evolution will continue in the future.

I have always loved children and was eager to start a family soon after getting married. But, little did I know then that my road to motherhood would be a long, unwinding one. We spent so long waiting for this joy, and were slowly starting to accept the reality as it was. Just then, my daughter arrived as the most precious gift of god almighty. Her arrival made me believe and slowly, yet mysteriously, made the pain of the past many years fade into the distant. Motherhood inspired me to reach for the stars and helped me explore this aspect of writing, i.e. poetry.

This book comprises poems expressing my learnings from all walks of my life. My focus has been on sharing useful insights in a poetic style with the readers. I hope these nuggets will inspire and guide the readers. Some poems are written to provide food for thought and stimulate the readers on important issues faced by all of us. Read these poems in your leisure time, while travelling or when you need inspiration. Read them one by one, or in a group of few. If these poems make even a few people smile and are found relatable by the readers, my purpose of publishing them will be fulfilled.

You Came in My Life

You came in my life, when I least expected it
You came in my life, when I was about to give up
this hope
You came in my life, and changed it forever
You came in my life, to make it complete

Doubts and negativities slowly left my heart and
mind, when
You came in my life
My pain and stresses melted little by little, when
You came in my life
You filled my heart with distinct joy and
contentment
I had never experienced till then
You came in my life, and brought back my belief

You came in my life and I was reborn everyday
You came in my life and I made choices everyday
You came in my life and inspired me
You came in my life and gave wings to the poet
hidden in me

Gratitude Fills My Heart

I count my blessings and notice others'
sufferings,
Gratitude fills my heart
I realise the privileges I have been born with,
And gratitude fills my heart
I weigh my blessings against my shortcomings,
And gratitude fills my heart
I value the merits of my near and dear ones
And gratitude fills my heart

So what do I do when gratitude fills my heart?

I give, give and give
I have so much to give and there's so little time
I give my time, my kindness and my smile
I give things material and otherwise, to make me
feel worthwhile
I give my silence, instead of hurtful words
I give my best wishes, my silent prayers hoping
to make people smile
I give as selflessly as I can
I give whenever I can

The more I give, the more I have to give
The more I give, the more I receive

As I keep giving, I keep becoming humble
As I keep giving, I keep becoming content

Designations

I search for myself amid a maze of designations
I seek pride and respect, through designations
I work hard day and night, to achieve a
designation
I play the games I need to, to achieve a
designation

I assess my skills against a designation
I seek to control others, through a designation
I take pride on achieving a designation and, yet,
I quickly start seeking a higher designation

I seek higher pleasures through my designation
I want to feel important through my designation
I attach myself to a designation

Oh, and then I face the harsh truth

Respect is of the designation, not me
Designations are temporary, just like oh little me
Strip me away of my designation, and the world
will forget me

Designations don't define me, my thoughts and actions do
Designations give me the chance to spread positivity and inspire people
In a way only I can do

As these realisations dawn upon me
I understand the illusion that designations really are

As I stop chasing them, I find myself

Me? A Writer?

Me? A writer?
At first seemed like a tall task
Me? A writer?
Is a question I still ask

My journey of writing started with my first job
Where I analysed industries, companies and
stocks
From writing scripts for videos to writing long
form features and one-on-one talks
I covered the entire gamut of write-ups on stocks

Then came the watershed moment
I started writing a wide variety of content
Reminding me of the question again
Me? A writer?
How? What? When?

Along came the pandemic, I started writing
versus in my mind
Me? A writer? Me? A poet?
The answer to this question became clearer with
time

The answer was hidden in the eyes of a little angel
Who inspired me to sing along
One lullaby, two lullaby, so many lovely songs
She inspired me to explore this angle

So here I am
Writing a poem or maybe it's a song?
Still unsure if I can call myself a writer
Me? A writer? Me? A poet?
Or maybe just someone trying to express her thoughts

I put my pen to paper and write my very first poem
The words start pouring like uncontrolled rain
The fluency surprises me, the joy is beyond measure

So, I continue expressing my purest emotions

Guruji

I read in Bhagavad Gita, "Everything is
temporary"
Yet, I never really understood its true meaning
I learnt, experienced and understood "Anitya"
from you guruji

Guruji, you gave my life a whole new direction, a
whole new meaning
Your pious voice guides me through life's thick
and thin
You cleared my mind of so many doubts and
confusions
You helped me break so many illusions

Your teachings help me stay strong during storms
Your words provide me motivation to go on
And clarity when haywire I have gone

Though I have never met you, I feel like I know
you
Over time, a debt has piled up that I owe you
Practicing your teachings is the only way
Through which tribute to you I pay

My heart holds gratitude unbound
For I am lucky enough to have you around
I send my metta and best wishes your way
As my heartfelt homage to you for showing me
the way

Words

Words, words, words
So easy to say, so difficult to weigh
Immense power they hold
To mend or end bonds, new and old

Words, words, words
Be mindful of what you say
Keep hearsay at bay
Our conversations small and long
Can stay with us for times prolong

Words, words, words
Write them down, or read them out
Grow their value by leaps and bounds
Write, rewrite and improvise
To slowly become more wise

Words, words, words
Use them with prudence
To heal, spread joy and make the heart dance
Avoid lies, gossip and unnecessary chatter
Become more peaceful and happier

Words, words, words
Difficult to count them or their forms
Yet silence can be so telling
Muting the words, escaping the storms

I Write

I write to express
I write to impress
I write to clear my mind
I write and calmness I find

I write on stocks
I write on trending talks
I write to earn a living
I write to continue giving

I write to feel joy and satisfaction
I write to stretch my limits
I write to decide a course of action
I write to reach a destination
I write to add value to my minutes

I write to know myself more
I write to explore
I write to become my best version
I write to achieve and avoid diversion
I write to pour out my grief
I write when I am full of joy

I write to take pride in my words
I write to connect with the world
I write forever, I write after breaks
I write to reduce the heartaches

I write, rewrite and edit
I write and delete
I write to publish my thoughts
I write to hide my thoughts

I write and become complete
I write, never to compete
I write and am grateful that I can
I write to venture into the new
I write and then I know I can

Entitlement

Sense of entitlement, can be misleading
Sense of entitlement, can lead to resentment
Sense of entitlement, is the biggest delusion ever
Sense of entitlement, is like a fever

Sense of entitlement, fosters craving and jealousy
Sense of entitlement, curbs empathy

Fall not in the trap of entitlement
It keeps you away from true enlightenment
A breeding ground for one's ego
Sense of entitlement, let it go

Sense of entitlement, can be blinding
It keeps you in the vicious circle, running

Entitled we are to nothing
Grateful we should be for everything
Sense of entitlement is like flowing water
No point running after

Writing and Me

Writing and me haven't always been on the
same side
It gave rise to fear of imperfection in me as a
child

As a student, writing was about mugging up and
penning endless words
The ones who wrote the most, scored higher, at
least that's what we were told

Writing and me started becoming friends
As my career slowly moved in that direction
Our love grew stronger over the years
As writing spilled over to my personal corridors

Writing and me, our bond stands the strongest
today
As we are not afraid to try new things everyday
I am grateful to have discovered this facet of my
personality
Coz writing helps me maximise my capabilities

You

You found me out of nowhere
You caught me unaware
You are the best surprise I have received
You are a precious birthday gift indeed

I thank you for choosing me
I thank you for completing me
You gave me the unparalleled joy of motherhood
You made me believe that I could

With you, I become better everyday
With you, I discover myself everyday
With you, I find peace
With you, I find ease

You turned my life around in a few days
You filled my life with illuminating rays

You grow up in a haste
I try to make most of every phase

You change every day
I look forward to every single change
I still can't believe you are mine
I give you all that I call mine

I love you, angel

I Close My Eyes

I close my eyes, I find myself
I look inside, I understand the world
I close my eyes, I unravel the reality as it is
I seek the truth, I find it one by one

I close my eyes, I find answers...
... to questions I asked and the ones I didn't

I close my eyes, I erase my defilements
I close my eyes, I fortify my merits
I close my eyes, I am filled with calmness
I close my eyes, I watch my tears wash away my
pain

I close my eyes, I become aware
With eyes shut, my mind opens
I observe myself like only a true Vipassi
meditator can

I close my eyes, I forgive one and all
I close my eyes, I seek forgiveness
I generate loving kindness for all beings
I share my merits with one and all

I close my eyes, I keep practicing regularly
I close my eyes, I walk the path diligently
With hopes of progressing towards my
destination
I keep focusing on the present

I try to show this path to many
I serve the dhamma to express my gratitude
I close my eyes, I open my heart

The Pain Melted Away

The first time I held you as mine
Out poured the rain, the pain melted away

First time you kissed me,
First few clicks with you,
First few times we were called mother and
daughter,
First time you communicated with me
Tears filled my eyes, tears of joy, tears of
disbelief
The pain melted away

Between naps and sleepless nights
Between nappy changes and feeding times
I embraced the role of motherhood
The pain melted away

Your smile
Your innocence
Your love
Your sweet gestures
Made the pain melt away

Never could I have imagined
Years of waiting, suffering and sadness could be
so easily wiped away
As I wonder in amusement
The pain melted away

I Look For Success

I look for success
Scoring high marks
Being among top 10 rank holders
Excelling in activities I loved
Becoming the class monitor

I look for success
Being loved by all
Having many friends, young or old, short or tall

I look for success
Being popular in college
Learning new life skills

I look for success
In earning more, in designations
By leading people
By honing my talent
By writing well

I look for success
In loving relationships
In raising my child well
In being there for people who matter

I look for success
In overcoming my weaknesses
In amplifying my strengths
In growing my merits
In dhamma

I know I will be successful
When I am at peace with myself
When I know myself
When I am content

The Burden of Attachments

The burden of attachments
We carry unknowingly
The burden of attachments
Is the root cause of all our sufferings

Wants, desires and endless wishes
I, me, myself, mine
We attach ourselves to things, large and sundry
We attach ourselves to all things impermanent
We attach ourselves to an illusion called "I"
We continue to live in this ignorance
And pile up a huge burden of attachments

Wake up, oh mankind, become aware
Light the lamp of truth, erase the despair
Detach, detach, detach
And make better decisions
Detach, detach, detach
And reduce your sufferings
Detach, detach, detach
And achieve heights of greatness

As you strengthen your detachment
Slowly, the burden reduces
Until one day you wonder
Oh, where is my pile of attachments?
Ah, I am finally free from the burden of
attachments
I am truly liberated and ready to fly

Let Go of the Ego

Look, my dear, look for the ego hidden within
Identify its root cause
And let go of the ego

Ego manifests within us in several forms
Some apparent, others camouflaged
I, me, myself – 3 words that ego feeds on
Blur these words, begin to transform

Anger is a key form of ego
It condescends others, "how come they don't know?"
Understand the truth behind anger
And become your own anchor

Ego spoils relationships
Ego makes one alone
Ego is nothing but a delusion
Let go of the ego

Empathy and gratitude
Build these within your heart and mind
And witness the ego lag behind

Ego is a barrier to excellence
Ego is a one-sided lens
Ego will never let you grow
Let go of the ego

Comfort Zone

Comfort zone can be tough to find
Comfort zone gives us some of the best times
Comfort zone has several merits
Comfort zone enlivens our spirit

Yet seek to break out of the comfort zone
Growth is seldom found in the comfort zone
Venture outside, where lies your true potential
Venture outside, understand you are special

Venturing into the unknown can be unnerving
Yet, it can be most self-serving

Seek to create comfort zones
When it's time, break out of comfort zones

Make and break comfort zones
Become more detached
Make your best decisions
Once you are detached

Keep exploring and rebuilding, my friend
You are a lot wiser and peaceful in the end

Giving

Nothing is more satisfying than giving
Giving makes life worthy of living
Giving provides the heart with wings
Giving helps us venture beyond material things

Giving is never big or small
Giving touches the lives of one and all
Giving has to be selfless
Giving with an impure mind, benefits the giver
much less

Giving can become a way of life
Giving can be of several kinds

Give because you are grateful
Give because you should
Give because you can
Give quietly, seek nothing in return

Equanimity

Equanimity is rare to find
Equanimity isn't always at the top of our mind
Equanimity is difficult to attain
Equanimity liberates us from our pain

Equanimity comes to those who seek it
Equanimity is built slowly and over time
Equanimity makes us calm during life's ebbs and
flows
Equanimity, persistent efforts help it grow

Equanimity makes us wiser
Equanimity enhances our karma
Equanimity is the key to liberation
Equanimity helps us face the toughest situation

Equanimeous, that's the way to be
Equanimity has merits plenty
Seek equanimity every single day
Equanimeous actions never let us sway

Identify the Ego

Identify the ego, it is the anger within
Identify the ego, it is the quest for recognition
Identify the ego, it is the need to have control
Identify the ego, it is an inner hole

Identify the ego, it is the want to become
biological parents
Identify the ego, it is the want to see self in our
children
Identify the ego, it is the corruption
accompanying power and position
Identify the ego, it is in everything we call I, me,
mine

Identify the ego, it is your biggest enemy
Identify the ego, it propels envy

Identify the ego, break out of its shackles
Identify the ego, conquer your inner battles

Power of Empathy

Empathy is more powerful than sympathy
Empathy does away with pity
Empathy should be practiced and developed
within us
Empathy brings out the best in us

When we empathise, we understand
When we empathise, we help to mend
When we empathise, we provide comfort to
others
When we empathise, we light a lamp inside us

Power of empathy cannot be overstated
Power of empathy is often underrated
Empathy has power to make us calm
Empathy has power to make us kind

So take a vow, to build empathy inside you
Empathy will help reduce negativities inside you

Who Am I?

Who am I?
Only wise ones seek answer to this question
Who am I?
Often it takes a lifetime to answer this question

Who am I?
Am I the relationship – a daughter, a wife, a
mother?
Am I the designation – researcher, writer, AVP?
Am I the gender – she/hers, they/theirs?

Who am I?
I am someone trying to live life on my own terms
I cannot be defined merely by my religion or
societal norms
I am someone looking to reach my full potential
I am someone looking to unravel all truths
existential

I am nothing but a culmination of all my karma
I am learning and imbibing rules of pure dhamma
I am but a human being bound to err
I am determined to become more aware

Metta

Metta is a Buddhist term meaning loving
kindness
Metta is a trait we all have, some have more,
some have less

Metta is a wonderful sentiment
Creating positive vibes, uplifting the
environment
Metta helps us reduce the effect of negativity
within us
Metta is a way to give back to the people around
us

Metta helps us let go of our hate
Metta helps us come out of our fears
Metta makes us realise we all are one
Metta makes us realise we can love everyone

Metta helps us amplify the love within
Metta benefits us and all other beings

Metta is most powerful when done with an
equanimeous mind
Metta helps us become purer, more kind
Strive we must to practice metta regularly
For then we will be able to care selflessly

Mudita

Mudita refers to unselfish joy
Mudita finds joy in others' happiness
Mudita might seem too good to be true
Mudita enhances life's satisfaction and value

Mudita is the counterpart of envy
Mudita helps us befriend many
Mudita helps us experience unadulterated joy
Mudita helps us become selfless and truly enjoy

Mudita is an inner spring flowing in us eternally
Tap into this spring and live life with greater self
sufficiency
Mudita curbs greed, helps us achieve greater
heights
Mudita helps us break the cycle of endless wants,
cherish life's delights

Life is too short for envy and jealousy
Practice mudita diligently
Cultivate the feeling of oneness
Learn to live in a state of true happiness

Ebbs and Flows

Ebbs and flows, are inevitable
Ebbs and flows, are uncontrollable
Ebbs and flows, make us strong
Ebbs and flows, teach us to come along

Fear not the ebbs and flows
Understand both come and go
Stay calm through both ebbs and flows
Stay observant of both ebbs and flows

Ebbs pose challenges
Stay fearless, have faith
Ebbs reveal the truth of beings near and dear
Ebbs make us wiser, make us understand who we
are

Flows seem easy
But hidden challenges they carry
Flows can inflate our ego, make us fly away
Don't get attached to flows, they will go away
someday

Accept the existence of ebbs and flows
Resolve to stay level headed as they come and go
Meditation is a tool to help you stay neutral
And observe the ebbs and flows from a distant
level

Explore the Grey

Black and White have long been in the limelight
But, seldom do we find hearts purely Black or
White
Explore the Grey, for its relatively unchartered
territory
Explore the Grey, for every heart has its own
Grey story

Grey is what makes us human
Identifying the Grey helps us become a better
human
Grey has a beautiful range of shades
Grey spans an array of emotions

Grey changes with different situations
Grey is yet one of the few constants

Explore the Grey, try to move into the light
Explore the Grey, that's where all the conflicts lie
Explore the Grey, aspire to clear the mind and
heart
Explore the Grey, let the conflicts die

Explore the Grey, in self and others
Explore the Grey, accept its existence
Explore the Grey, become more empathetic
Explore the Grey, coz its sometimes magnetic

Explore the Grey, increase your tolerance
Explore the Grey, stop seeking absolutes
Explore the Grey, get direction
Explore the Grey, undertake correction

Put Yourself First

Put yourself first, before reaching out to do a
greater good
Put yourself first, only a happy soul can make
others feel good
Put yourself first, to ensure your thoughts are
healthy
Put yourself first, stop spreading your negativity

Put yourself first, not your ego
Understand the difference between self-respect
and ego
Put yourself first, that's who you are answerable
for
Put yourself first, no one else will do it for you

Put yourself first, to bring out the best in you
Put yourself first, to know the complete you
Put yourself first, to put your best foot forward
Put yourself first, strive to make others happy

Put yourself first, avoid moving closer to
darkness
Put yourself first, achieve high finesse
Put yourself first, learn to let go
Put yourself first, forgive and forgo

Put yourself first, it's the right thing to do
Put yourself first, be helpful to others and be
true
Put yourself first, you will shine brighter
Shine brighter, spread the light all around you

Spirituality

Spirituality is different from religion
Spirituality lies within us, religion lies in books
written by humans
Spirituality encompasses all, religion confines
hearts within small walls
Spirituality is based on the eternal truth, defined
by god
Religion is based on rules formulated by humans,
is often a façade

Spirituality lies in our karma
Religion follows rites and rituals, not pure dhamma
Spirituality promotes curiosity of all kind
Religion is rigid and limits the mind

Spirituality gives us true inner peace
Religion sometimes makes humanity cease

Spirituality liberates us from binds of attachment
Religion fortifies attachment
Touch, looks, sound, taste and smell – spirituality
realises their impermanence
Touch, looks, sound, taste and smell – religious
practices propel these senses

Spirituality brings us closer to all beings, all
things natural
Religion breeds hatred, things inhuman

Embrace spirituality, discover the universal truth
Avoid spirituality, remain ignorant of the truth

Learning

Learn, be a student of life
Learn, coz there is very little time
Learn, make it a way of life
Learn, it helps you gain your rhyme

Learn, in deeds big and small
Learn, from one and all
Learn, it will make you content
Learn, it will help you reinvent

Learn, from mistakes of others
Learn, from books and verses
Learn, become efficient
Learn, become sufficient

Learn, you can seldom know it all
Learn, stand out and stand tall
Learn, and yet be humble
Learning stops when you think you have it all

Learn, do same things differently
Learn, do new things frequently
Learn, there's no other way to grow
Learn, never be driven by ego

Learn, and pass on your learnings
Learn, and share your earnings
Learn, and grow together
Learn, become wiser
Learn, develop gratitude

Colours of the Pandemic

The pandemic came out of the blue
It brought out multiple colours from us, all
shades of true

Blue was the colour of frontline warriors - doctors,
nurses, police officers and others
Their days seemed never ending, more
challenging than many others
Covered in protective gear from head to toe,
They fought many wars - experienced many
highs and lows
Some lost their lives serving others
Most stayed away from their families, battled
their inner pain and stress
I salute those who strived to save lives in times of
burgeoning distress

Red was the colour of this health crisis,
With many losing their lives to the virus
Lives were lost also for lack of livelihood
As the pandemic shut shops many, across the
global neighborhood

The pandemic brought to fore
Shades of grey and green, hidden within our core
Distrust, jealousy and fear stood tall
Distancing us from one and all
The so called weak emerged the strongest
As the virus sought company of the mightiest
Rumours, hatred and political games had a gala time
As the pandemic showed its might, one wave at a
time

White was the colour of a select few
Who reached out to others, just because they could
Such people overcame their fears
To spread love and faith among those near
I take inspiration in thee the common man
For extending a helping hand
I also did my tiny bit, to keep alive the human
spirit

I reflect on those times with awe and wonder
And feel grateful eventually mankind conquered
As the pandemic becomes endemic
It continues to create tales epic

Why Judge?

Why judge?
Are we credible enough to judge another?
Why judge?
Judging distances us from each other

Why judge?
Aren't all judgements temporary?
Why judge?
Our judgements are based on attachments so many

Why judge?
If judgements breed negativity inside us
Why judge?
If judgements make us angry and jealous

Why judge?
Focus on living our life, not analysing it
Why judge?
If judging makes us more impatient

Why judge?
Do we know their journey enough?
Why judge?
Do we know their roads have been extremely
rough?

Why judge?
Just because they are different?
Why judge?
Let us practice empathy, instead
Why judge?
Live and let live, move ahead

Why judge?
Become more accepting, more tolerant
Why judge?
Become a friend, a confidante

Parental Paradox

Parental paradoxes are real
They involve complexities galore
Making choices that seem to be ideal
Keeping everyone's best interests at the fore
Homemakers or career focused
These paradoxes parents can hardly avoid

Should I be strict? Should I let the innocent one
be?
I so enjoy the cute mistakes, oh, but I am
supposed to stop them
Ensuring she eats right? Ensuring she eats happily?
Going out with friends? Staying at home with the
little one?
Attending office meetings? Attending PTA
meetings?
Being her friend? Being her mother?

I traverse through such questions galore
Doing the best I can, hoping to do more

I often wonder though

Do these paradoxes affect mothers more?

Coz let's face it, responsibilities are titled towards
mothers at the core

Why are these choices easier for fathers?

Why do mothers face so many societal
pressures?

Stories

Stories, date back to time immemorial
Stories, come in different shades and can be
inspirational
Stories, weave their magic, are timeless
Stories, are passed on across generations

Short or long, different genres
Stories reflect so many cultures
Truth or fictional, educational or religious
Stories, leave an indelible mark on us

Stories, make us laugh and cry
Stories, make us curious
Stories, we follow them diligently
Stories are relatable, strike an emotional chord

Stories, act them out and get love of the masses
Stories, the best ones are also appreciated by the
classes

Stories, connect us with each other
Stories, come handy in all spheres
Stories, telling them is a special skill
Stories, our senses they fill

Stories and storytelling are everyone's' favourite
They can match multiple, varied wavelets
So here we go, passing stories to our next
generation
It's the easiest and most impactful way to impart
education

Script of Life

Script of life, we ourselves write
Our reactions often become the storyline
Script of life, is random and undefined
For seldom does life move in a straight line

Stay aware, coz life slips away, and how
The time to change the script is now
Script of life, write and rewrite
Coz we have, but this one life

Script of life, should give you joy and satisfaction
Script of life, embrace imperfections and pain
Script of life, create it by your own actions

Script of life, need not be in one genre
Script of life, write it in inks of all colours

Script of life, beware the end could come
anytime
Live every breath, make every moment prime
Script of life, memories are all you are left with
Script of life, your karma is what you live with

Seeking Validation

We seek validation
As a child from our parents, relatives and
teachers
As a teenager from our friends and peers
As a professional from our bosses, customers,
teams, partners
As a spouse from our better half and in-laws
As a parent from our children

We seek validation
From everyone who matters

Seeking validation
Is futile due to its impermanence
Seeking validation
Makes us vulnerable, breeds restlessness
Seeking validation
Limits us and our capabilities
Seeking validation
Limits our possibilities

Seek validation, if you must
By weighing your actions on the karma meter
By wiping your mind clean of all the dust
By ensuring you spread smiles, gain trust
By staying true to yourself and to others

The only validation you need
Is knowing you did all you could
Is being as selfless as you possibly could
Is ensuring the wellness of self and others

Feminism

Feminism, seeks equality for women
Feminism, a word heard often among
intellectuals
Feminism, a word gaining increasing prominence
Feminism, is defined differently by different
individuals

Is feminism
About defining women's roles?
Is feminism
About rating some women above others?
Is feminism
About blaming men unabashedly?
Is feminism
About just one gender?
Is feminism
About being politically active?

Feminism to me
Is about 'live and let live'
Is about freedom to choose
Is about true collaboration across genders
Is about accepting more, judging less

Feminism to me
Is about having equal opportunities
Is about being human, making mistakes
Is about standing up, for self and others
Is about celebrating different choices

Feminism is also about challenging irrational
beliefs
It is about embracing the new, asking questions
Feminism has miles to travel yet
The progress made so far is only minuet

I hope to live in a world
Where roles are not defined by gender
Where expectations are based on capabilities
Where people are free in the truest sense

God and Me

God and me
Have an ever evolving bond
As a child, I always thanked him unbound
For back then, everything I wanted, I found

Growing up, I started understanding more
I started making wishes for my loved ones
Slowly, my wish list expanded
To things material and divine

My faith in god has always been strong
Though I always questioned rituals we
performed all along
I knew all the stories and divine songs
I found peace in them, they made me feel
belonged

Then came the time
For the mystery to unravel
And all my doubts were dispelled
Seemed like god I had rediscovered

God resides inside each of us
His qualities are present inside each of us
These qualities might be underdeveloped or
hidden
Build on these qualities, let your story be
rewritten

True way to worship god is to follow his trail
Practice his teachings, abandon blind faith
All gods in all religions advocate the same things
Become empathetic, develop loving kindness
towards all beings
Rites and rituals will do us no good
Purify your mind, your karma, come out of the
woods

Emphasize not on stories or songs of god
Be aware of true virtues of god
Follow those virtues, develop them within you
That's when god will truly smile upon you
Stay human, let go of ego
Selfishness, attachment let them go

Expectations versus Hope

Expectations versus Hope

One adds burdens, other adds positivity

One chases desires, other is steeped in reality

One drives impatience, other is a soothing agent

Expectations versus Hope

One breeds sense of entitlement, other liberates

One is rigid, other more accepting

One we develop unknowingly, other we work
towards maintaining

Expectations versus Hope

One seeks fulfilment, other is open to
disappointments

One leads to incorrect decisions, other propels
careful consideration

One brings us misery, other brings us peace

One can lead to darkness, other exudes
illuminance

Expectations versus Hope
Choose wisely, my friend
Focus on bringing suffering to an end
Be realistic, be optimistic
Unfulfilled expectations can make you
pessimistic

Black Swan Events

Black swan events
Are rare and unpredictable by definition
Yet, off late they epitomise frequent uninvited
guests
Global pandemic, global wars, and the like create
several stress

Black swan events
Seem to have become a recurrence
Are making the world more resilient
Are making us value our existence

Black swan events
Bring out the best and worst of mankind
Bring the world together, polarise the minds
Brings us strength, as we fall and get up
determined

Black swan events
Cannot be just wished away
Can make us pray for a better day
Can continue to make the world sway

Black swan events
Are nature's way of restoring order
Are extremely trying for one another
Are unpredictable, cannot be prepared for

So let's vouch to stay together
Upheld humanity now and forever
For that's the way to emerge stronger
From black swan events, their impact lasts longer

You Are the Key

You are the key
To all your dreams
To your happiness
To your future

Change yourself
Its the easiest thing to do
No one will be as you ask them to
That's how you can add value

You are the key
Unlock all answers
Unlock your true potential
Unlock the truth within

Change yourself
And see the world afresh
And drive the new
And outgrow your shortcomings

You are the key
Put self-first
Turn on the inner light
Reach new heights

Impermanence

Impermanence, one big truth of life
Impermanence, in most things it resides
Impermanence, identify this truly
Impermanence, realise this and rise to glory

Seek permanence in things bound to change
Lose peace of mind, find pain
Understand the impermanent
Curb extreme, emotional reactions

Realisation of impermanence, a life changing
moment
Build on this, keep purifying your thoughts
Stay with impermanence, stay calm
Let go of the impermanence, keep adding to your
misery

Birthdays

Birthdays
Excite children the most
Involve celebrations galore
Make us feel special, cared for

Birthday celebrations
Are often limited to the privileged ones
Weaker sections find them cumbersome
Can sometimes go over the top
Can be used to benefit a larger lot

Don't jump up and down on each birthday
Coz your time on earth reduces with each
birthday
Not to say you cry on each birthday
Just count your blessings, be grateful on each
birthday

Birthdays
Use them to reflect back on life
Use them to identify the purpose of your life
Use them to make a difference in self and others'
lives

Mother's Love

Mother's love
Is as selfless as we humans can be
Is something that we all need
Gives us strength in the toughest times
Gives unconditionally, helps us find our rhyme

Mother's love
Knows no bounds
For some, it remains out of bounds
Few remain ignorant of its merits unbound

Mother's love
Comes in several shades
Can be white, black or grey
Seeks the best for her children
Doesn't fear taking the path less trodden

Mothers
Are humans like all of us
Often make mistakes
Are constrained by their own limitations
Give them room for some imperfection

Motherhood

Motherhood comes in different forms
Most women are biological moms
They bear immense physical and emotional
stress
They love their kids in times of joy and distress

Some though, stand out
Their motherhood is outside the usual norms

Motherhood, sometimes comes through adoption
For they, wait long and carry immense emotional
pain often

Some mothers are surrogates, their newborns
they give away
Such huge indebtedness, no amount of money
can repay

Some mothers come in pairs of two
They battle societal judgements to love their
little ones

Some mothers are single moms
Juggling multiple roles all on their own

All these mothers make difficult choices
They value motherhood much more than anyone
else
Learn to respect all mothers, irrespective of their
type
Coz a mother's love can never be defied

Stripped off Her Dignity

Stripped off her dignity
By animals disguised as men
Stripped off her dignity
By the society, thereafter, again and again

Stripped off her dignity
Some survive, some don't
Stripped off her dignity
This trauma lasts throughout her life

Stripped off her dignity
And yet she gets blamed
Stripped off her dignity
For no fault of hers, she feels ashamed

Stripped off her dignity
Scarred for life
Stripped off her dignity
Struggles with relationships for quite sometime

Stripped off her dignity
Experiences patriarchy deep rooted within our
minds
Stripped off her dignity
Struggles to live with her head held high

Stripped off her dignity
She needs lots of love and empathy
Stripped off her dignity
Give her some space, just let her be

Stripped off her dignity
Raise your sons right
Stripped off her dignity
Teach your daughters how to fight

Being Old

Being old
We fear it all our life
Isn't something we can avoid
Is an inevitable part of life

Being old
Has its own struggles
Has several positives too
Has been an evolving definition

Being old
Means you can relax
Means you are out of the daily race
Means you can enjoy your retirement

Being old
Brings with it health issues
Brings the pain of losing loved ones
Brings fears of being left alone

Being old
Brings the wisdom to see through the masks
Brings the reality of death closer everyday
Brings the true love and care of a few

Being old

Prepare for it, every way you can

Prepare for it, make a plan

Prepare for it, vow to make the best of those days

Conflicted

Never have I ever
Felt so conflicted
A life changing, surprise event
Shook my strong beliefs

A country where women are worshipped
A country where women endure tremendous
atrocities
Some killed in the womb
Others abandoned hours after being born
Throughout their lives
Several traumas they face

The yearning for boys
The aversion towards girls
I could never understand

Yet, here I stand gaining from such aversion
This development is a fateful one
Indicating our karmas are intertwined like none

So I live with this conflict
Delving into the depths of my mind
Hoping some day
A logical end this conflict might find

Rights and Wrongs

Rights and Wrongs
There aren't any, believe many
I agree with it, albeit partly

Rights and Wrongs
Don't exist in all subjective aspects of life
Living together with someone or on your own
Doing some work, or not
These choices are led by situations
These choices differ for every individual

Rights and Wrongs, though
Exist in their absoluteness
In matters of physical safety, wellness

It's wrong to beat or kill an innocent another
It's wrong to physically assault another
It's wrong to indulge in acts of sexual harassment
It's wrong to ignore above acts

It's right to strive for equality
It's right to stand up for yourselves
It's right to stop misdeeds of others and our own
It's right to ensure complete safety of one and all

Scars caused by wrongs can last lifelong
Help in healing them, receive love and respect
unbound
Support the wrongs, lose the ones affected, forever

Reinvent

Reinvent
Yourself
Your organisation
Your relationships

Reinvent
Repurpose
Evolve
Grow

Reinvent
Stay relevant
Become content
Be the best you can

Reinvent
It's a necessity
It will help you compete
It will take you places

Experiences

Experiences
Often define us
Sometimes blind us
Sometimes provide insights

Experiences
Can be good, bad and everything in between
Can make us an expert in somethings
Can drive us to extremes

Experiences
Mould them favourably by responding
Avoid thoughtless reacting
Try to observe them a bit distantly

Experiences
Leverage them to bring out your best
Ensure the learning you never forget
Not all need to be your own
Learn from those of others

Listening

Listening
Is often underrated
Is a skill that can be bettered
Is important in one's communication armour

Listening
Helps us connect better with each other
Enables us to have empathy for each other
Makes us strengthen our bonds with each other

Listening
Build this habit constantly
Teaches you more than incessant talking
Gives you direction and melancholy

Listening
Adopt it in good times and bad
It can help you become glad
Is not a convenient fad

When Our Gods Look Down

When our gods look down
Do they smile more or frown?
Do they feel proud or letdown?
Do they sense gloom all around?

When our gods look down
They see their devotees fighting each other, in
their names
They see hatred march over love
They see mankind steeped in distress

When our gods look down
They see the path shown by them is long
forgotten
They see distorted versions of their lessons
They see a select few owning religion

When our gods look down
They know spirituality has taken a backseat
They find few followers of pure dhamma
They find few people focused on their own
karma

Raising a Child

Raising a child
Is not a job mild
Can really churn our mind
Is not really defined

Raising a child
Can leave us beguiled
Can be distinctly styled
Can give us joy refined

Raising a child
Is about being there
Is about devoting our time
Is about learning life's rhyme

Raising a child
Isn't about being perfect
Is to care and protect
Is about building a strong connect

Journalists

Journalists
Seek truth in a maze of lies
Provide insights to untrained eyes
Some are looking to sensationalise

Journalists
Often drive positive societal change
Often work in ways strange
Often fall in dangerous range

Journalists
Are a passionate lot
May not make money a lot
Follow the trail of their thoughts

Journalist
I became one by chance
I overstayed perchance
I sometimes miss that dance

Girl versus Boy

Girl versus Boy
Is one a boon, other a bane?
Should they be distinctly trained?
Should one endure more pain?

Girl versus Boy
Are their roles predetermined?
Should they live in societal confines?
Can their lives they themselves design?

Girl versus Boy
Why is one judged more?
Why is the other favoured more?
Why is one always adapting more?

Girl versus Boy
Leave behind the biases
There aren't many differences
Embrace both with equal grace

Stay in the Present

Staying in the present
One of the toughest things to do
Brings out a new you
Provides a realistic view

Stay in the present
And make it count

Stay in the present
Past cannot be changed
Future cannot be prearranged

Stay in the present
Be present
Enjoy this present

Imperfections

Seeking perfection has its merits
Know, though, perfection often doesn't exist
Perfection can be completely subjective
Having different definitions in different contexts

Imperfections
Beautiful they can be often
Unfiltered thoughts they reflect often

Imperfections
Look beautiful in pieces of art
Provide a sneak peek into an author's thoughts
Bring out the innocence of a little tot

Imperfections
Are sometimes best left untouched
Are humane, not to be hushed
Make us more accepting and humble
Make us more empathetic to others

Imperfections
Can act as our guiding stars
Can help us improvise

Imperfections
Identify them
Accept them
Learn from them

Purpose

Purpose
Lose it, go haywire
Find it, aspire

Purpose
Is a necessity
Has high utility

Purpose
Define it, commence
Redefine it, maintain relevance

Purpose
Know the whys
Navigate the hows

Purpose
Drives us
Completes us

Purpose
Achieve it
Be satisfied

I see you
And my heart melts away
Your innocence makes my mind sway
I am filled with joy, my heart flies away

I see you
Your pretty, brown, almond shaped eyes
Your heart warming smile
Your cute face, your soft tresses
You leave me beguiled

I see you
Oh little one
You change every minute
Your curiosity knows no limit
You grow bit by bit
Your growth seems so rapid

I see you
And all your firsts
I feel blessed
To share these moments

I see you
You are a big piece of my heart
You and I will never be apart

Subtle Passion

Passion is the fire within
To achieve, to win
It is the constant drive
To excel, to thrive

Passion can be of two kinds
Aggressive and subtle
Both have their pros and cons
One though has more lows

Aggressive passion
Can expedite the rise
Can sharpen the fall

Subtle passion
Involves careful consideration
Involves gradual accession

Subtle passion
Is more peaceful
Is more graceful

Choose wisely, my friend
Choose to grow, to be enlightened

Punctuations of Life

Punctuations
Are found abound in books
Often define our life's nooks

Punctuations of life
Are signs waiting to be unveiled
Are tests of our resolve, our will

Full stops are the hardest to deal with
They arrive unexpected, break our myths

Commas help us enlist our blessings, joys, pains,
achievements many
Commas join instances together
Commas help us start a story

Question marks, several arise throughout our
lives
Initial ones are simple and easy to answer
They gain complexities as we grow older
Not all of them have an answer

Underline the learnings of life
Leverage the learnings of life
Underline all failures in life
For failures are teachers of life

Beware of quotation marks
They highlight importance of each spoken word
Hard can be the impact of the spoken word
Exercise caution while uttering every word

Exclamation marks express feelings strong
They often come out unannounced
Define moments of extreme pain or joy
Are expressions of the purest form

Ellipsis have a special utility
Deploy them to ignore all the noise
Do this, stay focused, enjoy

Avoid the Noise

Noise pollutes minds, not just air
The unnecessary gossiping
Over-the-top drama, ego boosting
The attention seeking
Different forms of noise these are

Avoid the noise
In all arenas of life
Avoid the noise
Stay focused, take greater strides

Avoid the noise
It holds little merit
Avoid the noise
Give yourself relief
Avoid the noise
It's not worth your time

Love

Is love
What we see in Indian movies?
What we read in novels?
What we dream about as teens?

Love
Is about caring silently
Is about giving selflessly
Is about being there, constantly

When you love someone
Accept them as they are
Keep expectations at par
Keep negativities afar

Love yourself
To truly love another
To stay happy together
To make each other better

Silence

Silence
Is an unsung force
Has merits galore
Must be practiced more

Silence
Reconnects us with our inner voice
Helps us identify and avoid the noise
Is a wiser choice

Silence
Volumes it can speak
Assent and dissent, both it can depict
Provides direction in times bleak

Silence
Sometimes carries immense pain
Sometimes propels injustice, sins
Sometimes must be broken, for greater gain

You and I

You and I
Are completely opposite personalities
Are joined together by our destinies
Are helping evolve each other's individualities

You and I
It's been a roller coaster ride
Have conquered every tide
Never left each other's side

You and I
Almost drifted apart
Doubts flooded our hearts
None believed we could play our parts

You and I
Have come a long way
Yet, sometimes, it feels just about halfway
Sometimes, we sway away

You and I
Are in a comfort zone
Are the 'different' ones
Have together grown

You and I
I still seek your validation
I still feel something is missing
I still wonder am I doing all I could?

You and I
I wish you expressed more
I read your actions to know your core
I hope your soul you would pour

You and I
I have left nothing unsaid
I seek a little more respect
I look forward to the road ahead

Am I Doing Enough?

Am I doing enough?
I keep asking this question to myself
I want to give my best to all who matter
I want to be as selfless as I possibly could

Am I doing enough?
To spread positivity around me?
To bring small joys around me?
To keep knowing and evolving the real me?

Am I doing enough?
To stay focused?
To stay empathetic?
To stay real?

Am I doing enough?
I ask, to
Reassess my moves
Identify my errors
Rectify my errors

Am I doing enough?

Keep asking this question to yourself

Often all answers you will find within yourself

Will keep you more loving towards others

Alive Again

You came into our world
And we feel alive again
Your smile, your innocence, your pure world
Make us feel alive again

With you, every experience is new
And we feel alive again
With you, we have lots to look forward to
And we feel alive again

Without you, life was passing us by
With you, we feel alive again
Without you, we were combating the pain
With you, we feel alive again

You made the pain melt away
And we feel alive again
You fill our hearts, give us joy
And we feel alive again

You give us hope, new aim
And we feel alive again
You complete our lives
We love you with all our hearts
And we feel alive again

Stand Up for Yourself

Stand up for yourself
It's the right thing to do
None other will do it for you
Be ready for the new

Stand up for yourself
Build a quiet resolve
To make negativities dissolve
To continuously evolve

Stand up for yourself
Don't tolerate injustices
Don't give in to your weaknesses
Don't give power to others' sicknesses

Stand up for yourself
Put yourself first
Refuse to be coerced
Use your full force

What's Real?

In this world full of virtualism
In this world full of pretension
In this world full of masked men and women
Ask, my friend,
What's real?

Amid the unnecessary gossip
Amid the 'he says', 'she says'
Amid the constant chase for ego gratification
Ask, my friend,
What's real?

Look within, find your demons
Look within, fight your demons
Look within, know the impermanent
Ask, my friend,
What's real?

Is it social media
Is it so-called friends
Is it the curious kind
Ask, my friend,
What's real?

Materialistic gains
Social reputations
Mortal remains
Ask, my friend,
What's real?

Our True Love

Our parents
Our siblings
Our spouse
Our children
Our families
Our friends
Who, my dear, is our true love?

Our work
Our passion
Our hobby
Our duty
What, my, dear, is our true love?

Our egos
Our aspirations
Our goals
Our needs
Our wants
Ourselves, indeed, are our true love

Know the eternal truth
Know the depth of self-love within
Know that we are our true love

Start evolving
Start achieving breakthroughs
Start becoming selfless
By knowing who is our true love

The Sustainability Agenda

Mother earth suffers from the excesses of
mankind
Human wants outnumber natural reserves,
destroy all they find
Excessive capitalism endangers our dear planet
Yet many of us refuse to change our ways

Voices supporting nature are getting stronger
Together they are making forces, standing longer
Talks, promises, commitments fill every nook
and corner
Yet, the actual impact remains smaller

Sustainability is another business opportunity for
many
Sustainability is giving rise to new employment
opportunities
Sustainability initiatives are being adopted by
many
Seriousness and urgency of these issues is
understood by a few only

Nature has time and again displayed its immense might
The pandemic forced humans to stay inside
Let us resolve to care for mother earth
Let us get serious, look beyond our own girth

Analysing Life

Analysing life
Just how much is enough?
Are we doing it too much?
What should be its purpose?

Analysing life
Is important
Enables growth
Helps us evolve

Analysing life
Look inward, not outward
Look at self, not others
Look at the forest, not the trees

Analyse life
But don't stop living it
But do it with a focused sight
But have the greater good in mind

I Wonder

I wonder
How come my sincerest efforts went vain?
Why did I witness a distinct betrayal, pain?
Why did I try so hard, again and again?

I wonder
Why my efforts seem one sided?
Why am I being blamed?
Why they prefer to stay blinded?

I wonder
Why I still long to belong?
Why I still hurt, exert?
Why I still feel sad?

I wonder
Why should I endear the ignorant?
Why should I endure injustice?
Why should I pretend?

I wonder
Is it better to just accept the truth?
Is it better to make peace with the loss?
Is it better to stay at bay?

I wonder
Why do I still care?
Why are people still unfair?
Why do I pray for a repair?

I wonder
When will I stop resenting the hate I get?
Will I ever truly forgive and forget?
Will I ever feel truly at peace with the facts?

In the end, this realisation dawns upon me
Somethings are just not meant to be
I make peace with this reality
I move on with agility

Reacting or Responding

Reacting or Responding
What are you doing?
Which propels misdoing?
Which one should you be adopting?

Reacting or Responding
One reckless, other thoughtful
One vents, other converses
One brings stress, other resolves

Reacting or Responding
Make your choice wisely
Chose peace of mind over the petty
Explore the whole world of possibilities

Silent Supporters

A successful woman
Receives support from many
Spouse, family, friends, house helps plenty

A successful man
Has always been supported
By his mother, sister, wife

Then
Why does the support given by women go
unrecognised?
Why are the homemakers taken for granted?

Silent supporters
Women have been forever
Doing their part dutifully, over and over

Silent supporters
Must be celebrated
Should not be under rated

Silent supporters
Must be identified
Must be acknowledged
Must be respected

A Householder Hermit

Staying calm
Is easier in isolation
Is enriching through meditation
Is key to self-purification

A householder hermit
Is hard to find
Stays calm in the daily grind
Focuses on purifying the mind

A householder hermit
Tries to minimise attachment
Seeks to enhance contentment
Stays with people, practices selflessness

A householder hermit
Is spiritually inclined
A fine balance finds
Always keeps greater good in mind

A householder hermit
Fulfills all responsibilities diligently
Aspires to evolve consistently
Looks at the forest, not the trees

Lockdown Tales

Lockdown tales
Are galore, across the yore
Are white, black and grey
Are unique in their own way

Lockdown tales
Emerged during a rare event
Multiple ways they went
Will live on forever

Lockdown tales
Are different for different people
Are memories penal, unforgettable
Are all things human, bring out the inhuman

Lockdown tales
Are yours and mine
Don't follow a straight line
Are both devil and divine

Lockdown tales
Carry invaluable lessons
Remember them, live the lessons
Forget them, live in ignorance

Lockdown Memoir

Lockdown
Came out of nowhere
Was an event unimagined, rare
Gave us a deep glare

Lockdown
Emotions grew strong
Often felt like a sentence, stretching long

Lockdown
Slowly we discovered its merits galore
Spending time with family, doing more

Lockdown
Brought to fore hidden skills
Some artistry, some delicious meals

Lockdown
Broke longstanding myths
Saw surprisingly high productivities

Lockdown
Brought many health scares
Families stayed together...
.... Distance failed to stop the cares

Lockdown
Pushed compassion in front seat
People helped each other feel complete

Lockdown
Watching Netflix
Playing board games
Meditating more

Lockdown
Yearning to travel
Sometimes being fearful
Sometimes feeling worried

Lockdown
Enhanced the feeling of gratitude
Redefined many redundant attitudes
Made us value our people more

Lockdown
We ventured beyond our fears
We served people in ways newer
We used the opportunity to volunteer
We used to make our hearts purer

Craving and Aversion

Craving and Aversion
Reside deep inside us
Should be reduced
Bring misery to us

Craving and Aversion
I write to drive awareness
I write not to propel these
I write to share my learnings

Craving and Aversion
Work towards resolving them
Meditation is a tool to avoid them
Practice regularly and overcome them

Craving and Aversion
My guruji enlightened me
I thank him profoundly
Walking his trail will set us free

Love Songs

Love songs I have been hearing forever
Most of them propel yearning for those dear
Love poems also do the same
Keep us bound in attachment's chains

Its time love songs are reimagined
Its time love songs get real
Its time love songs propel selflessness
Its time love songs highlight love that liberates

I love songs about true love
I love songs that dive deep into human psych
I love songs that talk of loving kindness
I love songs that present love's beautiful reality

Love can change destinies if it liberates
Love can give so much if it's selfless
Love can make the world a better place
Love can propel mankind into greatness

I Surrender

My heart and soul
I surrender
To your innocent world
Oh, my little doll

I love your ways
Of discovering
Of loving
Of erring

I give in
To your caresses
To your punches
To your kisses

I live
Every moment with you
Every moment like you
Every beat of you

I feel complete
I feel alive
I feel blissful
Just being with you

So I surrender
To you in whole
You enrich my soul
You teach me so much, my love